Crime and Punishment

Kathy Elgin

Illustrated by Adam Hook

CHERRYTREE BOOKS

First published in paperback in 2009

Published in Great Britain by Cherrytree
Books, part of the Evans Publishing Group.
2a Portman Mansions,
Chiltern Street
London W1U 6NR

Produced for Evans Brothers by
Bailey Publishing Associates Ltd
11a Woodlands
Hove BN3 6TJ

Editor: Alex Woolf
Designer: Simon Borrough
Artwork: Adam Hook
Picture research: Glass Onion Pictures

British Library Cataloguing in Publication Data
Elgin, Kathy, 1948
    Crime and Punishment - (Shakespeare's
    world)
    1. Shakespeare, William, 1564-1616 -
    Themes, motives - Juvenile literature
    2. Crime - England - History - 16th
    century - Juvenile literature
    3. Crime - England - History - 17th
    century - Juvenile literature
    4. Punishment - England - History - 16th
    century - Juvenile literature
    5. Punishment - England - History - 17th
    century - Juvenile literature
    6. Criminology - England - History - 16th
    century - Juvenile literature
    7. Criminology - England - History - 17th
    century - Juvenile literature
    8. Great Britain - History - Elizabeth,
    1558-1603 - Juvenile literature
    I. Title
    364. 9'42'09031

ISBN 978 1 842 34539 9

Printed and bound in China

Titles in this series:
Daily Life
Crime and Punishment
Health and Disease
Theatre and Entertainment

Picture Acknowledgements:
The publishers would like to thank the follow-
ing for permission to reproduce their pictures:
Art Archive: 4 and cover inset (Musée du
Château de Versailles / Dagli Orti), 6
(Bibliothèque des Arts Décoratifs, Paris / Dagli
Orti), 12 and cover background (British
Museum / HarperCollins Publishers), 16
(Biblioteca Nacional, Madrid / Dagli Orti), 19t
(British Library, London), 23.
Bridgeman Art Library: 9t, 10, 15t, 15b (Roy
Miles Fine Paintings), 17 (Victoria & Albert
Museum, London), 19b, 24 (Monasterio de El
Escorial, Spain).
Mary Evans: 9b, 20.
Shakespeare's Globe Picture Library: 29 (Andy
Bradshaw).
Topham Picturepoint: 7 (Fotomas), 11, 13, 21
(Fotomas), 22 (Museum of London), 25, 27l
(Fotomas), 27r (Woodmansterne), 28 (Royal
...).

Contents

Introduction

Who Was Shakespeare?

William Shakespeare is probably the most famous playwright in the world. He was born in 1564 in Stratford-upon-Avon, and four hundred years after his death his plays are still being performed all over the world in almost every language you can think of. Although he came from a fairly ordinary family and didn't even go to university, he wrote thirty-eight plays with exciting plots and new, dramatic language.

Most of his plays were performed at the Globe, one of the very first theatres in London. Some were also performed for Queen Elizabeth I herself at court. Because he was also an actor and probably appeared in some of his own plays, Shakespeare knew what audiences liked. He became one of the most popular playwrights of his day and, by the time he died in 1616, he was a wealthy man.

Crime and Punishment in Shakespeare's Time

There was a lot of crime in Elizabethan England. Part of the problem was poverty. There were no social services in those days, and many people were forced to steal money or food simply to stay alive. But it was also to do with the way the Elizabethans thought about society. They liked a calm and settled way of life and this depended on everyone behaving themselves and being content to remain in their own proper place.

Most people lived their whole lives in the village or town where they were born and worked for the local landowner. They were very suspicious of strangers, especially if they were poor or unemployed. Anyone who disturbed the peace was considered a threat to society and had to be punished. Homeless people and beggars in particular were regarded as criminals, even if they had not committed any particular crime.

Crimes like murder and treason were, of course, very serious and deserved proper punishment. Many people, however, were punished harshly for things that we consider quite trivial — stealing bread, perhaps, or just being out on the street at night. There were a lot of complicated laws and a wide range of quite brutal punishments, some of which seem more like torture to us.

Shakespeare had seen beggars wandering the countryside when he lived in Stratford. When he moved to London he saw pickpockets and other thieves in the streets. All these types of people found their way into his plays.

Vagrants, Beggars and Outcasts

Vagrants, or vagabonds, were people who had no home or job. They wandered about the countryside, surviving by begging for food and money. They were usually servants who had been dismissed, or wounded soldiers unable to work. There were also orphan children and women deserted by their husbands. People were afraid of beggars because they often travelled in large groups and sometimes became violent.

Disabled beggars got more sympathy. Some had genuine war wounds, but others injured themselves – or their children – on purpose.

> *… like silly beggars*
> *Who, sitting in the stocks, refuge their shame,*
> *That many have and others must sit there.*
> RICHARD II, ACT 5, SCENE 5

silly: simple, defenceless
refuge: shelter from

The law said that poor people had to be supported by the parish. Nobody wanted to pay to support vagrants, of course, so local residents always wanted them moved on. But before that they had to be punished. The penalty for begging was to be put in the stocks and then tied to the back of a cart and whipped out of town. Constables went round the streets at night, looking in all the taverns for homeless people. All those who could not prove that they had a home were rounded up and brought before the law in the morning.

what I do, to spite the world.

People came out onto the street to watch and jeer as vagrants were whipped out of town.

> … *I am one, my liege,*
> *Whom the vile blows and*
> *buffets of the world*
> *Hath so incens'd, that I*
> *am reckless what*
> *I do, to spite the world.*
> MACBETH, ACT 3,
> SCENE 1

liege: lord
buffets: knocks
incens'd: angered
reckless: careless

The person most feared was the "masterless man", one who had no job and no respect for the law. They often appear in plays, called "malcontents". In real life they were outcasts from society and were often forced to become criminals. The man who speaks here is someone to whom so many terrible things have happened that he no longer cares what dreadful deeds he does to get his own back. Because of this, he has agreed to commit a murder for Macbeth.

Society was very divided, with a huge gap between rich and poor.

Thieves and Footpads

There was a whole underworld of professional criminals. They even had their own language, a kind of slang called "Peddlar's French". A "nipper" cut off purses from people's belts. A pickpocket was called a "foist", "priggers of prancers" were horse thieves, and "coney-catchers" were swindlers who tricked people out of their money. The crowded city streets swarmed with these rogues. An Italian visitor to London wrote "There is no country in the world where there are so many thieves and robbers as in England …".

… he daily doth frequent
With unrestrained loose companions,
Even such, they say, as stand in narrow lanes
And beat our watch and rob our passengers.
RICHARD II, ACT 5, SCENE 3

frequent: associate
loose: immoral
passengers: travellers, passers-by

Pickpockets only stole money or handkerchieves. They rarely attacked anyone violently.

Bolingbroke is talking about his young son Hal, the future King Henry V, who is involved with bad company. In the narrow streets, mugging was common, especially after dark. Gangs of men hung about waiting to set upon unwary travellers or drunks returning late from the tavern. Nervous citizens could hire a "linkboy" with a torch to light them safely home. In the countryside, highwaymen were a constant danger.

loose companions, Even such,

> *Alas, what danger will it be to us,*
> *Maids as we are, to travel forth so far?*
> *Beauty provoketh thieves sooner than gold.*
>
> As You Like It, Act 1, Scene 3

Above: Nicholas Jennings was a notorious coney-catcher, who would disguise himself both as a ragged beggar and a respectable citizen.

Women travelling alone were particularly at risk. Rosalind and Celia decide that one of them should dress as a boy for safety on their journey to the Forest of Arden. A relatively harmless trick was for vagrants to hold up rich people and steal their clothes. They then dressed them in their own rags, made their getaway, and later sold the good clothes for money. This is one of the comic scenes in *The Winter's Tale.*

Highwaymen held people up at gunpoint and shot those who resisted. Because of this, they were hanged when caught.

Murderers

Murder has always been considered the worst of all crimes. It was punishable by death, usually by hanging. Murders in the course of robbery were common. Elizabethan constables often found bodies in the street in the morning. But Shakespeare also shows us murders committed for more complicated reasons. Ambitious people like Macbeth want to get rid of their rivals. The conspirators murder Julius Caesar because he is ambitious, while Othello kills his wife out of jealousy. Although he shows us why the characters behave as they do, Shakespeare usually makes it clear that murder is a terrible sin.

> *Murder most foul, as in the best it is;*
> *But this most foul, strange and unnatural.*
> HAMLET, ACT 1, SCENE 5

The ghost of Hamlet's father has come to tell him that he was murdered. Even worse, the murderer was his own brother. The ghost cannot rest until he is revenged. This became a popular theme in Elizabethan plays, where revenge was presented as an honourable thing. All too often, though, it just provoked more murders, both in plays and in real life. Many family feuds, begun with a single murder, went on for generations.

Julius Caesar was stabbed to death by Brutus and other men he believed to be his trusted friends.

like Pilate would I wash my hands

> *A bloody deed, and desperately dispatch'd.*
> *How fain, like Pilate, would I wash my hands*
> *Of this most grievous murder.*
> RICHARD III, ACT 1, SCENE 4

fain: willingly

Richard III has just had his brother Clarence killed — one of the many murders Richard has engineered in order to become king. Other victims include his two little nephews, the princes in the Tower. There were some famous real-life murder scandals at the court of Elizabeth I, one of them involving Robert Dudley, Earl of Leicester. He was the queen's favourite but very unpopular with everyone else. He was suspected of having murdered his wife, Amy Robsart, in order to marry the queen.

Richard III sent murderers to smother the two princes but made sure to stay out of the way himself.

In the world of Elizabethan court rivalry, stabbing or poisoning often put a swift end to a quarrel.

Treason

Treason was the crime of plotting against the king or queen. Because the monarch was believed to be God's representative on earth, it was like committing a sin against God. Treason almost always carried the death penalty. There were several attempts on the lives of monarchs in Shakespeare's day. In 1594 Queen Elizabeth's doctor, Roderigo Lopez, was accused of trying to poison her. In 1605 Guy Fawkes and his fellow plotters attempted to kill King James I. Shakespeare's early history plays, about the Wars of the Roses, include many treacherous attempts to overthrow the government.

> *Treason and murder ever kept together, As two yoke-devils sworn to either's purpose.*
>
> HENRY V, ACT 2, SCENE 2

yoke-devils: devils working together
either's: each to the other's

Henry V has discovered that three of his most trusted men have been conspiring with the French enemy to kill him. He has all three executed immediately. Queen Elizabeth dealt just as harshly with plotters in real life. When the Earl of Essex's rebellion failed in 1601, the queen had him executed, even though he had always been one of her favourites. Foolishly, Essex had announced his intentions by organizing a performance of *Richard II*, which shows a king being overthrown.

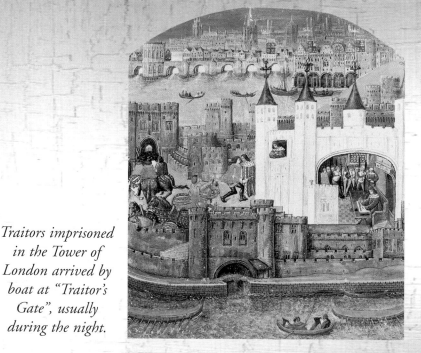

Traitors imprisoned in the Tower of London arrived by boat at "Traitor's Gate", usually during the night.

> *Though those that are betray'd*
> *Do feel the treason sharply, yet the traitor*
> *Stands in worse case of woe.*
>
> CYMBELINE, ACT 3, SCENE 4

Supporters of Mary Queen of Scots' claim to the English throne were declared traitors. Mary herself was beheaded in 1587.

Traitors were despised and feared by everyone. The Elizabethan government had its own secret service under Sir Francis Walsingham. His network of spies operated throughout the country, gathering information on anyone suspected of plotting against the queen. Traitors were sent to the Tower of London, where they could be imprisoned for years before finally being executed. Often they were tortured in the room under the White Tower. The only hope for anyone convicted of treason was to beg for a royal pardon, but this was rarely granted.

Prisoners stretched on the rack usually confessed or betrayed their companions.

As two yoke-devils sworn to either's purpose.

13

The Watch

In Shakespeare's time there was no official police force. Instead they had the watch. These were patrols of armed citizens under the command of a constable. The watch were the first layer in the system of law and order, and they kept the peace on a local level. When they caught anyone misbehaving, they arrested them and took them to a magistrate to be questioned and dealt with. The watch carried considerable authority and because of this they were generally feared and disliked.

The sheriff and all the watch are at the door; they are come to search the house. Shall I let them in?
HENRY IV, PART 1, ACT 2, SCENE 4

In this quote the watch are pursuing Falstaff after a robbery. When a crime was committed, it was up to ordinary citizens to raise the alarm — the "hue and cry". This meant shouting and generally making a noise to attract attention. Everyone then had to chase after the criminal. The watch would take over as soon as they were alerted. If a thief was caught with stolen goods on him, he was convicted on the spot.

Although everyone joined in the hue and cry, thieves often managed to escape in the narrow, crowded streets.

you are to bid any man stand, in the prince's name....

14

You are thought here to be

Because there was no street lighting, the bellman carried a lantern so that he could see and be seen on his night patrol.

> *You are thought here to be the most senseless and fit man for the constable of the watch; therefore bear you the lantern. This is your charge: you shall comprehend all vagrom men; you are to bid any man stand, in the prince's name.... You are to call at all the ale-houses, and bid those that are drunk get them to bed.*
>
> MUCH ADO ABOUT NOTHING, ACT 3,
> SCENE 3

senseless: sensible
fit: suitable
comprehend: apprehend, arrest
vagrom: vagrant

In this quote, Constable Dogberry, despite getting his words wrong, explains the duties of the watch. Most towns had a curfew, meaning that everyone had to be off the streets by about ten o'clock. In London, the city gates were locked at dusk. The watch were armed with heavy sticks, a spiked pole known as a "brown bill", a bell and a lantern.

The watch was made up of ordinary townsmen, elected by the town council and responsible to the sheriff.

Justice, Law and Mercy

The government passed laws to regulate almost every aspect of people's lives. You could be fined for not going to church on Sunday, for eating meat instead of fish on a Friday, or for failing to turn out for archery practice. People took each other to court for quite trivial reasons. Yet all these laws were treated with great seriousness by the courts. People began to depend on the strict definition of the law rather than on common sense, and this sometimes led to injustice.

Any accusation made against a person had to be proved in court.

fear: frighten
custom: familiarity

The Doctor of Law, in his long, black gown, was a highly respected figure.

We must not make a scarecrow of the law,
Setting it up to fear the birds of prey,
And let it keep one shape, till custom make it
Their perch, and not their terror.
MEASURE FOR MEASURE, ACT 2, SCENE 1

Because there were so many laws, people became expert at finding ways round them. When this happened, the laws were reissued and made harsher, as Angelo recommends here. Laws about public morality and those controlling vagrants were constantly being updated. Sumptuary laws, which said that only certain people were allowed to wear particular kinds of clothing, were revived many times since their introduction by Henry VIII.

> *The quality of mercy is not strain'd,*
> *It droppeth as the gentle rain from heaven*
> *Upon the place beneath: it is twice bless'd;*
> *It blesseth him that gives and him that takes.*
>
> THE MERCHANT OF VENICE, ACT 4, SCENE 1

strain'd: forced

Not many real court cases were as grand as this trial scene from The Merchant of Venice, *but surviving documents tell us a lot about Elizabethan law.*

Shakespeare is more interested in the human aspects of justice than in the law itself. He says that showing compassion to other people is usually better than simply depending on the rules. In *The Merchant of Venice*, a clever lawyer tries to persuade a vengeful man to show mercy after he has won his case. He refuses but is punished himself when the lawyer turns the tables and uses the same legal argument against him. Elizabethan law could be just as strict in reality. If you failed to make your case against someone you had accused, you could be penalized yourself.

The Courts

The Elizabethan legal system was complicated and very strict. There were at least eight categories of law and each crime was tried in a different kind of court. Simple cases like theft were tried locally by a Justice of the Peace. Serious crimes were tried twice a year by jury at the assize court under a judge appointed by the queen. Anything to do with moral behaviour or religion was dealt with by the ecclesiastical or church courts.

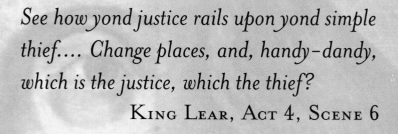

See how yond justice rails upon yond simple thief.... Change places, and, handy-dandy, which is the justice, which the thief?

KING LEAR, ACT 4, SCENE 6

yond: yonder, over there
rails: abuses
handy-dandy: make your choice

King Lear is saying that people should not take advantage of their position to judge others harshly. Through him, Shakespeare is arguing for a fairer society. Most Elizabethans were poor and badly educated. If someone was accused of a crime, he was compelled to appear in court at the risk of losing his house or his goods. Every man was expected to know enough about the law to defend himself in court, but the poor were always at a disadvantage.

Justices also met at the Quarter Sessions (four times a year), where convicted criminals could appeal against their sentences.

and beard of formal cut, Full of wise saws

… And then, the justice,
In fair round belly, with good capon lin'd,
With eyes severe, and beard of formal cut,
Full of wise saws and modern instances…
      AS YOU LIKE IT, ACT 2, SCENE 7

justice: Justice of the Peace
capon: chicken
saws: sayings
instances: examples

Above: Mary Queen of Scots was put on trial at Fotheringhay Castle in 1586 after the discovery of a plot against Queen Elizabeth.

Lawyers and justices were always men and came from the middle or upper classes. Because the law was so complicated, it was a rapidly growing profession. By 1586 there were 1,700 lawyers in Britain. Lawyers were unpopular because they made a good living out of people's misery and were suspected of taking bribes. After a rebellion in Shakespeare's *Henry VI*, the mob leader says: "The first thing we do, let's kill all the lawyers"!

The rather grand and formal Court of Wards and Liveries dealt with the inheritance of land.

Prison

Prison was not a punishment in itself. People accused of crimes were imprisoned until they were tried, found innocent and released. If they were found guilty, they were kept there until their punishment could be carried out. Others were kept locked up because they were too dangerous to be on the loose in society. There were no fixed sentences. Anyone arrested for debt, for example, had to stay there until he could pay it off. Playwrights found themselves locked up, too, usually because their plays were considered scandalous.

I take it, by all voices, that forthwith
You be convey'd to the Tower a prisoner;
There to remain till the king's further pleasure
Be known to us …

HENRY VIII, ACT 5, SCENE 3

There were at least eighteen prisons in London, each for different offenders. The Tower was for treason, Newgate was the main criminal prison, and Ludgate was the place for debtors. The Counter, open all night to take in people arrested by the watch, was usually full of drunken brawlers. The Fleet, the Marshalsea and the Gatehouse were for better-off folk charged with crimes against the state less serious than treason. The Clink was mainly reserved for those suspected of being practising Catholics, which was forbidden.

Most towns had a prison of some sort, just a sturdy, lock-up building where prisoners were kept before being sent to the nearest city for trial.

These prisoners at Newgate, arrested on religious charges, look quite respectable and have been allowed to associate with each other.

Some of Shakespeare's Measure for Measure *takes place in a grim prison, with characters under sentence of death.*

> *I have been studying how I may compare*
> *This prison where I live unto the world …*
> RICHARD II, ACT 5, SCENE 5

The most dangerous prisoners were chained to the wall by leg-irons.

Prisons were cramped, unhealthy places with few windows and little fresh air. They were also expensive – you had to pay to get in and out, as well as for lodging. The rich might have a room to themselves. The less fortunate shared with three or four others and probably shared a bed. Those who could not afford to have their own food cooked in the prison kitchens made do with charity food from the "alms-basket". These were bits of food collected from people in the street and taken back to the prison all mixed up together.

Punishment

Most Elizabethan punishments were physical and rather gruesome. The authorities tried to make the punishment suit the crime in some way. For example, a thief could have his hand cut off, or someone convicted of slander might have his tongue slit. Anyone who refused to plead either guilty or not guilty was pressed to death with enormous weights placed on their chest.

> *... his father had never a house but the cage.... I have seen him whipped three market-days together.... But methinks he should stand in fear of fire, being burnt i' the hand for stealing of sheep.*
>
> HENRY VI, PART 2, ACT 4,
> SCENE 2

cage: lock-up cage in the market place
methinks: I think

People had their ears or hands cut off or their noses slit just for stealing bread, let alone sheep. These injuries marked them out as criminals. For the same reason, first offenders were branded with "F" for felon, like the person in this quote. Next time they were caught, they were punished more harshly. In London, felons were chained to the river bank until the tide had washed over them for three days, which usually meant they drowned.

Hand-crushers were used to make people confess to their crimes or to cripple the hands of the convicted.

But methinks he should stand in fear of fire, being

> *... I was like to be appre-*
> *hended for the witch of*
> *Brainford. But that ... my*
> *counterfeiting the action of*
> *an old woman delivered me,*
> *the knave constable had set*
> *me i' the stocks, i' the com-*
> *mon stocks, for a witch.*
>
> THE MERRY WIVES OF
> WINDSOR, ACT 4, SCENE 5

Standing in the pillory was even worse than the stocks, where at least people could sit down.

apprehended: arrested
counterfeiting: pretending, imitating
delivered me: got me off

The real penalty for witchcraft was much worse: women were burned, hanged or drowned. Women who poisoned their husbands were also drowned, while male poisoners could be "boiled in water or lead", as one writer records. The stocks were reserved for fairly minor offences like drunkenness, rowdy behaviour, owing money or telling lies. People were usually left in the stocks, or the pillory, for a day or so.

Joan Prentice and two other women were publicly hanged as witches in Chelmsford, Essex, in 1589.

Shame and Hellfire

Public opinion was very important to the Elizabethans. The authorities realised that, for most people, being shamed in public was sufficient punishment for minor offences. People were paraded through the streets so that everyone could see and make fun of them. There was something, however, that Elizabethans feared even more than a public shaming. This was hell. People believed that hell was a real place where they would be punished for their crimes, even if they had got away with them on earth.

> *O, I were damned beneath all depth in hell*
> *But that I did proceed upon just grounds*
> *To this extremity.*
>
> OTHELLO, ACT 5, SCENE 2

were: would be
but: except
extremity: outcome

In the bottom right corner damned souls are suffering in hell, shown as the mouth of a huge monster. Paintings like this were a terrible warning!

Othello has murdered his wife. His excuse is that he genuinely believes her guilty of betraying him. Otherwise he knows that he would be punished in hell. Many other characters in Shakespeare's plays also refer to hell, especially those who have committed murders. Richard III and Brutus in *Julius Caesar* are both haunted by the ghosts of those they have murdered, who remind them of the terrible punishment to come.

> *Fellow, why dost thou show me thus to th' world?*
> *Bear me to prison, where I am committed.*
>
> *I do it not in evil disposition,*
> *But from Lord Angelo by special charge.*
> MEASURE FOR MEASURE, ACT 1, SCENE 2

committed: put in custody

The scold's bridle was a cruel punishment for women, who were often accused of being "unruly" when they were really just speaking up for themselves.

Claudio here does not want to be shamed by being led through the streets on his way to prison. There were other ways of shaming people. Anyone accused of immoral behaviour had to stand in church dressed in a white sheet. Women who talked too much or spread scandal had to wear a scold's bridle, a metal helmet which stopped them from speaking. In country districts, the "Skimmington Ride" mocked hen-pecked husbands. Villagers dressed up as the couple and paraded outside their house, acting out quarrels and beating pots and pans.

Villagers mocked their quarrelsome neighbours by making "rough music" outside their house.

Fellow, why dost thou show me thus to th' world? Bear me to prison.

25

Execution

Hangings were frequent and were carried out in public. They were not meant as entertainment but as a warning to those who watched. However, many of Shakespeare's characters joke about executions, suggesting that they were just part of everyday life and not particularly shocking. In London the main execution spot was at Tyburn, where Marble Arch is now. The worst criminals were hanged until they were almost dead, then cut down and their bodies cut into quarters. After that the internal organs were cut out and burned while they were still alive to watch.

Even the most skilled executioner did not always manage to sever the head at the first stroke.

… shall there be gallows standing in England when thou art king?

Thou shalt have the hanging of the thieves and so become a rare hangman.

HENRY IV, PART 1, ACT 1, SCENE 2

rare: excellent

As executions were quite expensive, local magistrates sometimes waited until they had several prisoners who could be hanged at once. Altogether, about a thousand people a year were hanged in England and Wales. Many others managed to get a reprieve by bribing the local sheriff, who was responsible for seeing that executions were carried out.

O Lord, Receiue my spirite.

In the 1550s the Catholic Queen Mary had hundreds of Protestants burned alive. Burning was still common for religious offences, as well as for witchcraft.

Some guard these traitors to the block of death,
Treason's true bed and yielder-up of breath.
HENRY IV, PART 2, ACT 4, SCENE 2

Instead of hanging, aristocratic prisoners accused of treason usually had their heads chopped off with an axe. This was considered a privilege, a concession to their status. Some were allowed to substitute a sword for the axe. Henry VIII, Queen Elizabeth's father, ordered the execution of Elizabeth's mother, Anne Boleyn. Later, Elizabeth had her rival Mary Queen of Scots executed in the same way. The execution blocks were on Tower Hill and Tower Green, inside the Tower of London. The heads of traitors were stuck on poles and left standing on the south side of London Bridge.

In the Tower of London the execution block and axe used to execute many people can still be seen.

Banishment

The punishment for serious crimes against the state, for anyone lucky enough to escape execution, was to be banished. This meant that the convicted person had to leave England and live abroad. Sometimes this was for a set period, or, in more serious cases, for life. For the aristocracy, being banished from court was almost as bad. When the Earl of Essex was dismissed from Queen Elizabeth's court in 1599, he immediately lost his influence in society and all his privileges. He was threatened with poverty and ruin.

> *Five days do we allot thee for provision*
> *To shield thee from disasters of the world;*
> *And on the sixth to turn thy hated back*
> *Upon our kingdom: if on the tenth day following*
> *Thy banish'd trunk be found in our dominions,*
> *The moment is thy death.*
> KING LEAR, ACT 1, SCENE 1

allot: assign
trunk: body

The Earl of Essex was handsome and dashing, but reckless. Although the queen pardoned him for many offences, he was eventually executed for treason.

The Earl of Kent is being banished unfairly. Because of this he takes a great risk, ignores his sentence and stays in England. He then returns in disguise to help the king who banished him. He also seems to have no family, which is good because banishment hurt the whole household. It interfered with the inheritance of property as well as splitting up husbands, wives and children.

Romeo finds out from the friar
that he is to be banished.

> Ha! Banishment? Be merciful, say —
> death;
> For exile hath more terror in his look,
> Much more than death. Do not say —
> banishment.
>
> ROMEO AND JULIET, ACT 3,
> SCENE 3

Romeo has been banished from Verona for killing one of the duke's family in a duel. He has only been banished to a nearby city but it is enough to separate him from Juliet. This shows how much people feared being separated from home and their familiar surroundings. Sending aid to a banished family member while they were abroad was forbidden. Since exiled foreigners were regarded with suspicion, they might therefore have no means of making a living.

Banishment meant severe hardship or destitution for the family left behind.

29

Timeline

1533   Princess Elizabeth, daughter of King Henry VIII, is born.

1536   Henry VIII passes a law allowing the branding of beggars.

1554   Under Queen Mary, Roman Catholicism is re-established in England.

1558   Elizabeth becomes queen.

1563   Laws are passed against witchcraft.

1564   Shakespeare is born.

1572   A law is passed by Parliament for the punishment of vagrants, including travelling actors.

1576   Another Act of Parliament establishes houses of correction and hard labour for vagrants and thieves.

1577   Sir Francis Drake sets off on his voyage around the world.

1580   New building in London is forbidden in an attempt to restrict the growth of the city.

1587   Mary Queen of Scots is executed after being implicated in a plot to kill Queen Elizabeth.

1594   Poor grain harvests increase the price of bread, the main food of the poor.

1596   Laws against vagrants are enforced, ordering the punishment of people with forged papers.

1597   A law is passed for the punishment of "Rogues, Vagabonds and Sturdy Beggars".

1598   New poor laws are introduced to take care of the poor. Another law places London vagabonds under martial law (policed according to military rules).

1599   Laws are passed against piracy.

1600   Statutes against vagabonds and the use of handguns are enforced.

1601   Poor law statutes compel each parish to provide work for the unemployed. London vagabonds are again placed under martial law.

1603   Queen Elizabeth dies and is succeeded by James I.

1605   5th November: the Gunpowder Plot to blow up Parliament is exposed.

1612   Witchcraft trials in Pendle, Lancashire, condemn many women to burning.

1616   Shakespeare dies.

Glossary

Further Information

Difficult Shakespearean words appear alongside each quotation. This glossary explains words used in the main text.

assize court	A sitting of the principal court in each county.
branding	Burning with a red-hot iron.
convicted	Found guilty.
felon	Someone who has committed a serious crime.
footpad	A robber on foot.
highwayman	A robber on horseback.
Justice of the Peace	A non-professional magistrate responsible for keeping the peace in his area.
magistrate	An officer concerned with the administration of the law; another name for Justice of the Peace.
malcontent	Someone discontented or at odds with society.
martial law	Law maintained by the army.
parish	A local area with its own church.
reprieve	Postponement or cancellation of a sentence.
slander	Saying bad or untrue things about another person.
stocks	A wooden structure with holes for the legs that was used as a form of punishment for petty crimes.
swindler	A cheat.
Tower of London, the	The royal palace, fortress and prison on the River Thames.
treacherous	Likely to betray.
treason	The crime of plotting against the monarch or government.
vagabond	A tramp or wandering, homeless person.
Wars of the Roses	A series of wars fought between the families of York and Lancaster (1455–1485).
White Tower, the	The central building in the Tower of London.

Further Reading

A Day in the Life of a Tudor Criminal by Alan Childs (Wayland, 1999)

Rebels, Traitors and Turncoats by Travis Elborough (Watling St, 2003)

Highwaymen, Outlaws and Bandits by Travis Elborough (Watling St, 2003)

The Elizabethan Underworld by Gamini Salgado (Sutton, 1984)

Eyewitness: Shakespeare by Peter Chrisp (Dorling Kindersley, 2002)

Shakespeare and the Elizabethan Age by Andrew Langley (Treasure Chest, 2000)

The Usborne World of Shakespeare by Anna Claybourne (Usborne, 2001)

What the Tudors and Stuarts Did for Us by Adam Hart-Davis (Boxtree, 2002)

The Best Loved Plays of Shakespeare by Abigail Frost and Jennifer Mulherin (Cherrytree Books, 1997)

Shakespeare's Storybook by Patrick Ryan (Barefoot Books, 2001)

Shakespeare Stories (two volumes) by Leon Garfield (Puffin Books, 1997)

Video, DVD and CD-ROM

All Shakespeare's plays are available in several versions from the Royal Shakespeare Company. These, and plays by other Elizabethan dramatists, can be ordered from their website (see below).
Complete Works of Shakespeare on CD-ROM (Focus Multimedia)

Websites

http://elizabethan.org/compendium/index.html
Life in Elizabethan England. Covers many aspects of daily life, including money, religion, fashion and food.

www.englishhistory.net/tudor.html
Tudor England. Contains information about Tudor history, daily life, and the lives of the monarchs. Includes an image gallery, eye-witness accounts and biographies.

http://www.eyewitnesstohistory.com/punishment.htm
Crime and Punishment in Elizabethan England.

www.rsc.org.uk
www.shakespeare.org.uk
Shakespeare Birthplace Trust. Contains background information on Shakespeare, his life and times.

Index